P9-DIJ-193

Behold the Beautiful
DUNG BEETLE

Cheryl Bardoe

Illustrated by Alan Marks

Charlesbridge

Somewhere in the world *right now* an animal
is lightening its load—

in your backyard,
on a nearby farm,
in a forest,
on a grassland far away.

Animals take nutrients from the food they eat.
Then, after their food is digested, they push waste
out in the form of dung, also called feces or poop.

Nearby, antennae detect the scent of dung in the breeze. One animal's waste is the dung beetle's treasure.

Dung beetles act fast when they sense the presence of dung. Protective top wings—called elytra—pop up. Broad flight wings frantically flap. Beetles race to the dung by the thousands. The first may arrive fifteen seconds after the dropping plops to the ground.

For these beetles, dung is a precious pile
of food and drink.

Bacteria live in the water that dampens dung, filling this fluid with protein and nutrients. Dung beetles use their paddle-like jaws to squeeze these rich juices out of the dung and into their bellies. The dung provides all the water and nourishment they need.

All dung beetles scramble to get a piece
of dung-pat pie fresh from the oven.
But each of the three types of dung beetles
has a different way of enjoying the poop.

Dwellers dig right in!

Dwellers hurry to eat their fill before the feces that caused the fuss dry out or disappear.

Rollers push perfect spheres of dung
away from the throng.

Rollers eat as they work, their jaws and legs moving nonstop to sculpt awkward clumps of dung into smooth, spinning balls. Then they balance upside down on stout front legs and use their back legs to steer the balls away from the dung pat. They want this dung all for themselves. The largest rollers, which are about the size of tennis balls, can roll dung balls up to fifty times heavier than themselves.

Tunnelers hoard their treasures directly
below the dung pat.

Tunnelers also eat as they work, stashing as much dung as possible in burrows beneath the dung pat. Females do the digging and make hundreds of trips to transport the dung deep underground. Males bring the females more dung and guard the entrances to their stockpiles against intruders.

Competition can be fierce.

Rollers engage in head-to-head
combat to defend their dung—
and for the promise of finding a mate.

Male rollers knock legs and heads to become king of the dung mountain. Winners attract mates while losers flail on bulky backs.

Tunnelers push and pry and twist and turn in underground battles.

Male tunnelers tussle to keep a burrow—along with the female and the dung stored inside. The bigger beetles, with larger horns, usually force smaller beetles out of nests and away from dung supplies. Females, who spend most of their time making nests, have either small horns or none at all.

Dwellers scuffle to keep their seats
at the table while the dung lasts.

Dwellers feast on the dung pat even as others try
to carry or stow it away, but they don't fight to
defend it. Being less choosy about the freshness
of their dung, many dwellers simply remain at
the buffet longer than other dung beetles. After
mating, they lay their eggs right in the dung.

Champions reap rewards.

Male rollers speed away with a
ball of dung and a female.

Female rollers skitter along behind the dung ball, help pull it, or catch a ride on it. When the rollers find soft soil in a secluded spot, they bury the dung.

Some rollers divide their day's earnings into several brood balls, while some make only one. After mating, the female lays a single egg inside each brood ball. The male moves on to find his next banquet, while the female hovers close, cleaning harmful mold off each brood ball before it can reach the precious egg inside.

Tunnelers mate and stash their eggs deep inside underground vaults.

Tunnelers may create up to fifty brood balls in the tunnels of their burrow. Most lay one egg for each brood ball. Some stick around, eating extra dung from their stockpiles while tending their brood balls. Others seal the nest with soil and then depart, watching and waiting for their next meal to fall.

The dung was once unwanted waste.
Now it is fuel for new life. . . .

Buried dung enriches the soil. Plants draw
nutrients from the dung into their roots, stems,
leaves, flowers, and fruits. The dung will also
supply nourishment for the beetles' offspring.

Eventually grubs hatch out of the eggs.
They eat and eat and grow and grow.

Young beetles, called grubs, have enormous appetites. Roller and tunneler grubs hollow their brood balls. Dweller grubs eat dried-up dung that adult beetles left behind.

   Later, as adults, the beetles will dodge birds, bats, and reptiles as they search for their next meal. But for now, whether above ground or below, the grubs are nestled in dung, which repels most predators.

One day the grubs stop eating and turn their energy inward. Their bodies transform.

As a grub grows, its protective outer covering, called an exoskeleton, becomes tight and must be shed. After this has occurred several times, the grub becomes a pupa. From the outside, the pupa appears to rest. Inside, its legs, body, and head reshape themselves. When done, the pupa sheds its exoskeleton one last time and emerges as an adult.

Just as butterflies emerge with wet, crumpled wings—adult dung beetles first appear as soft, pale shadows of their true selves. Little by little they begin to shine.

Brand new adult beetles are fragile. They remain safe in the dung until their elytra harden into shiny armor.

Clad in splendor, dung beetles ascend
into our world. They are ancient symbols
of life and renewal.

Ancient Egyptians were impressed with dung beetles, which they called scarabs. The orbs of dung that were rolled across the earth and buried reminded them of the sun traveling across the sky and setting into the horizon. Adult beetles crawling from the buried dung reminded them of the sun being reborn each morning.

Behold the beautiful dung beetle!

Finding Dung Beetles

Dung beetles are found on every continent except Antarctica. They can live in many habitats because all they need to thrive is a steady supply of the right kind of dung and soft soil in which to make nests. Although dung beetles have occasionally been found under doggie doo, they prefer the dung of herbivores, or plant-eaters. Dung beetles are attracted to droppings from animals as small as rabbits to those as big as elephants. The larger the dropping, the more beetles it attracts.

In the United States the best places to look for dung beetles are under cow patties or deer droppings. The bacteria that live in dung can make people sick, so use a stick or wear gloves when overturning droppings. And even if you don't think you touched any dung, wash your hands afterward, just to be safe.

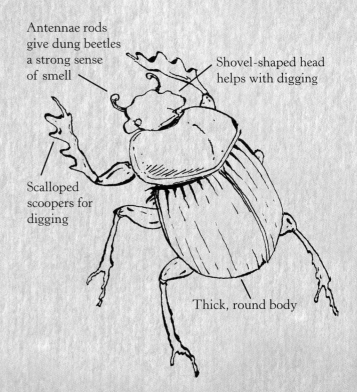

Antennae rods give dung beetles a strong sense of smell

Shovel-shaped head helps with digging

Scalloped scoopers for digging

Thick, round body

Fascinating Facts About Dung Beetles

- Scientists have identified more than five thousand species of dung beetles.
- Dung beetles don't eat their own dung. Their dung is very small, and it consists of the parts of their food that their own bodies couldn't use.
- Elephant dung attracts the most, and the largest, dung beetles—sixteen thousand beetles can divvy up a heaping helping of 3.3 pounds (1.5 kilograms) of elephant dung in two hours. Smaller beetles can make a cow pat disappear in twenty-four hours. However, some dung pats last for days, depending on the environment and the number and types of beetles nearby.
- Cattle are not native to Australia, so neither are beetles that eat cow dung. When European settlers brought the first cows to Australia in 1788, bush flies found cow dung to be a perfect breeding ground. Over time the cow herds grew—and so did the swarms of flies. Also, many pastures became carpeted with dung pats, which could take up to four years to decay. Scientists finally solved both problems in 1965, by importing dung beetles that specialize in eating cow dung.

Glossary

brood ball: A ball of dung that provides food and a safe place for young dung beetles to grow.

dung: The solid waste that comes out of an animal's body after it has digested its food.

dung pat: A heap of dung created by a cow, elephant, or other animal.

dweller: One of the three types of dung beetles. Dwellers live and lay their eggs in a dung pat, rather than moving dung to a nest.

elytra: The pair of protective wings that cover a beetle's more fragile flight wings.

exoskeleton: The tough outer covering that supports the bodies of some animals, including insects.

feces: See *dung.*

grub: The larva of a beetle.

larva (pl. larvae): A young insect that has recently hatched from its egg.

nutrients: The substances plants and animals need to grow and be healthy.

poop: See *dung.*

predator: An animal that hunts other animals for food.

pupa (pl. pupae): An insect during the stage of its life when it is transforming from a larva to an adult.

roller: One of the three types of dung beetles. Rollers roll balls of dung away from a dung pat before burying them in the ground.

tunneler: One of the three types of dung beetles. Tunnelers make their nests by digging tunnels directly below a dung pat.

waste: Unwanted, useless material.

Selected Bibliography

Evans, Arthur V., and Charles L. Bellamy. *An Inordinate Fondness for Beetles.* Berkeley, CA: University of California Press, 2000.

Lockwood, Sophie. *Beetles.* Mankato, MN: The Child's World, 2008.

White, Richard E. *A Field Guide to the Beetles of North America.* Boston: Houghton Mifflin, 1998.

The illustrations in this book show *Kheper nigroaeneus* (rollers), *Proagoderus rangifer* (tunnelers), and *Oniticellus egregius* (dwellers).

For my dear Hamline friends, who value children's books so much that they won't mind having a literary work about poop-eating insects dedicated to them
— C. B.

For Tori Poland

— A. M.

The author and illustrator gratefully thank Dr. Douglas Emlen of the University of Montana-Missoula for sharing his expertise in the development of this book.

Published by Charlesbridge
85 Main Street
Watertown, MA 02472
(617) 926-0329
www.charlesbridge.com

Library of Congress Cataloging-in-Publication Data
Bardoe, Cheryl, 1971–
    Behold the beautiful dung beetle / Cheryl Bardoe; illustrated by Alan Marks.
        p. cm.
    Includes bibliographical references.
    ISBN 978-1-58089-554-5 (reinforced for library use)
    ISBN 978-1-60734-620-3 (ebook)
 1. Dung beetles. I. Marks, Alan, 1957– II. Title.

QL596.S3B36 2014
595.76′49—dc23   2012038692

Printed in Singapore
(hc) 10 9 8 7 6 5 4 3 2 1

Illustrations done in watercolor and pencil on Fabriano 5 paper
Display type set in NeueNeuelandTF by TreacyFaces, Inc.
Text type set in Horley Old Style MT by The Monotype Corporation, plc
Color separations by KHL Chroma Graphics, Singapore
Printed and bound September 2013 by Imago in Singapore
Production supervision by Brian G. Walker
Designed by Diane M. Earley